Stage 2 Pack A

Floppy's Phonics Fiction

Kate Ruttle

Group/Guide

Contents

Introduction	2
Phonic focus	3
Vocabulary	4
Comprehension Strategies	5
Curriculum coverage charts	6

The Zip
Guided or group reading	10
Group and independent reading activities	11
Speaking, listening and drama activities	12
Writing activities	13

Posh Shops
Guided or group reading	14
Group and independent reading activities	15
Speaking, listening and drama activities	16
Writing activities	17

Bang the Gong
Guided or group reading	18
Group and independent reading activities	19
Speaking, listening and drama activities	20
Writing activities	21

Jack
Guided or group reading	22
Group and independent reading activities	23
Speaking, listening and drama activities	24
Writing activities	25

Quiz
Guided or group reading	26
Group and independent reading activities	27
Speaking, listening and drama activities	28
Writing activities	29

A Robin's Eggs
Guided or group reading	30
Group and independent reading activities	31
Speaking, listening and drama activities	32
Writing activities	32

Introduction

Welcome to *Floppy's Phonics!* This series gives you decodable phonic stories featuring all your favourite *Oxford Reading Tree* characters. The books provide the perfect opportunity for consolidation and practice of synthetic phonics within a familiar setting, to build your children's confidence. As well as having a strong phonic focus, each story is a truly satisfying read with lots of opportunities for comprehension, so they are fully in line with the simple view of reading.

Phonic development

The *Floppy's Phonics* Stage 2 stories support a synthetic phonics approach to early reading skills and are fully aligned to *Letters and Sounds*. They should be used for practice and consolidation. The books should be read in the suggested order (see chart on page 3), so that children can benefit from the controlled introduction, revision and consolidation of the phonemes. They can be read before the *Floppy's Phonics Non-fiction* books at the same stage. In addition, they can be used for practice and consolidation after introducing the sounds with other programmes.

The series can be used within the beginning of Phase 3 of *Letters and Sounds*, to support children as they broaden their knowledge of graphemes and phonemes for use in reading and spelling. The books will help to embed these vital early phonics skills, and help to ensure that children will experience success in learning to read and thus will be motivated to keep on reading.

Your children will benefit most from reading *Floppy's Phonics* Stage 2 if they are able to:

- recognize the graphemes introduced in *Letters and Sounds* Phase 2
- recognize the consonant digraphs from *Letters and Sounds* Phases 2 and 3
- blend and segment CVC words, including consonant digraphs (e.g. *shop*)
- recognize the *Letters and Sounds* high frequency words for Phase 2 and begin to recognize some for Phase 3.

Phonic focus

This chart shows which phonemes are introduced and practised in each title.

Title	ORT Stage Book band colour Year group	*Letters and Sounds* phase	Phonemes introduced	Phonemes revisited
The Zip	Stage 2 Red Reception	Phase Three	j w y z zz	
Posh Shops	Stage 2 Red Reception	Phase Three	x ch sh ng	
Bang the Gong	Stage 2 Red Reception	Phase Three		j w y ng ch sh
Jack	Stage 2 Red Reception	Phase Three	qu	j x ch sh
Quiz	Stage 2 Red Reception	Phase Three	th	w x ch qu ng
A Robin's Eggs	Stage 2 Red Reception	Phase Three	v	w ch sh th ng qu

Vocabulary

Most of the common words introduced in *Floppy's Phonics* are phonically decodable, using phonic skills and knowledge that are gradually developed through the stories. *Floppy's Phonics* also introduces the high frequency words which are listed in *Letters and Sounds*. High frequency words are common words which occur frequently in children's books. Many of them are decodable, some of them are 'tricky'. The words are defined in line with *Letters and Sounds*.

High frequency (HF) decodable words

Many of the high frequency words are decodable by saying and blending the sounds, and children should practise them regularly so that they can read them automatically as soon as possible.

High frequency (HF) tricky words

Some of the high frequency words are 'tricky', that is, they contain unusual grapheme-phoneme correspondences (e.g. *we, they*). The advice in *Letters and Sounds* is that children should be taught to recognize the phonemes they know within these words and to distinguish these from the tricky bits. For example, in the word *they*, children should be taught to recognize the grapheme *th* and then taught the tricky sound of 'ey' in this context.

Context words

In most of the books in *Floppy's Phonics* there are one or two other words, including the characters' names, which cannot be read using phonics alone, but which add to the child's enjoyment and understanding of the story. These words are listed as 'context words'.

The characters in these books are Mum, Dad, Biff, Chip, Kipper, Gran and Floppy. The names of the characters are listed as context words if they are not yet decodable.

The table on page 5 shows the context words, and the Phase 3 high frequency decodable and tricky words which appear in each story.

High frequency and context words used in each book

The Zip	HF decodable words	will
	HF tricky words	he, was, that
	Context words	–
Posh Shops	HF decodable words	with, this, will
	HF tricky words	was, her, you
	Context words	Gran, Kipper, Floppy
Bang the Gong	HF decodable words	will, them, this
	HF tricky words	you, was, her, we, be, she
	Context words	Kipper
Jack	HF decodable words	had a as on in big dad
	HF tricky words	me, was, has
	Context words	Kipper, FLoppy, cock-a-doodle-do
Quiz	HF decodable words	this, with
	HF tricky words	me, was, has
	Context words	Kipper
A Robin's Eggs	HF decodable words	with, will
	HF tricky words	they, are, her, we, she, see
	Context words	Mrs May

Comprehension Strategies

Reading is about making meaning, and it is particularly important that a child's earliest reading books offer opportunities for making meaning and telling a complete story. As with all *Oxford Reading Tree* stories, the titles in *More Floppy's Phonics* are fun stories which children will really enjoy, and which will give you lots of scope for practising and extending their comprehension skills.

Story	Comprehension strategy taught through these Group/Guided Reading Notes				
	Prediction	Questioning	Clarifying	Summarising	Imagining
The Zip	✓	✓	✓		✓
Posh Shops	✓		✓	✓	✓
Bang the Gong	✓	✓	✓		✓
Jack	✓	✓	✓	✓	
Quiz	✓	✓	✓		✓
A Robin's Eggs	✓		✓	✓	✓

Curriculum coverage chart

> **Key**
>
> **C** = Language comprehension   Y = Year   P = Primary
>
> **W** = Word recognition   F = Foundation/Reception
>
> In the designations such as 5.2, the first number represents the strand and the second number the individual objective

	Speaking, Listening, Drama	Reading	Writing
The Zip			
PNS Literacy Framework (YF)	1.1 2.1, 2.2 3.1	**W** 5.1, 5.2, 5.4 5.5, 5.8, 5.9 5.10 **C** 7.1, 8.1, 8.3	10.1
National Curriculum	working towards level 1		
Scotland (CfE) (P1)	Early level: LIT 0-01A/M/ LIT 0-02A/L/LIT 0-03A/V/LIT 0-04B/C/LIT 0-05D	Early level: LIT 0-01a/LIT 0-11a/LIT 0-20a/ENG 0-12a/ LIT 0-13a/LIT 0-21a/LIT 0-14a/LIT 0-07a/LIT 0-16a	Early level: LIT 0-01a/LIT 0-11a/ LIT 0-20a/ENG 0-12a/LIT 0-13a/ LIT 0-21a
N. Ireland (P1)	Attention and Listening: 1, 4, 5 Phonological Awareness: 2, 5 Social use of language: 3, 4, 5 Language and thinking: 1, 2, 4, 5, 6, 7, 11	Reading: 1, 2, 4, 5, 6, 7, 8, 11, 12 Progression: 1, 3, 4, 5	Writing: 1, 3, 4, 6 Progression: 2, 3, 4, 7
Wales (Foundation Stage)	Skills: 1, 2, 3, 5, 6 Range: 3, 4,5, 6, 7	Skills: 1, 2, 3, 4, 5, 6, 7, 8 Range: 1, 2, 3, 5	Skills: 1, 2, 3, 4, 6, 8 Range: 1, 2, 3, 4, 5

Curriculum coverage chart

	Speaking, Listening, Drama	Reading	Writing
Posh Shops			
PNS Literacy Framework (YF)	1.1 2.1, 2.2 3.1, 4.1	(W) 5.1, 5.2, 5.4, 5.5, 5.10 (C) 7.1, 8.1	9.1
National Curriculum	working towards level 1		
Scotland (CfE) (P1)	Early level: LIT 0-01A/M/ LIT 0-02A/L/LIT 0-03A/V/LIT 0-04B/C/LIT 0-05D	Early level: LIT 0-01a/LIT 0-11a/LIT 0-20a/ENG 0-12a/ LIT 0-13a/LIT 0-21a/LIT 0-14a/LIT 0-07a/LIT 0-16a/ ENG 0-17a	Early level: LIT 0-01a/LIT 0-11a/LIT 0-20a/ENG 0-12a/LIT 0-13a/LIT 0-21a/ LIT 0-21b/LIT 0-26a
N. Ireland (P1)	Attention and Listening: 1, 4, 5 Phonological Awareness: 2, 5 Social use of language: 3, 4, 5, 6 Language and thinking: 1, 2, 4, 5, 6, 7, 11 Extended Vocabulary: 2	Reading: 1, 2, 4, 5, 6, 7, 8, 11, 12 Progression: 1, 3, 4, 5	Writing: 1, 3, 4, 6 Progression: 2, 3, 4
Wales (Foundation Stage)	Skills: 1, 2, 3, 5, 6, 12 Range: 3, 4, 5, 6, 7	Skills: 1, 2, 3, 4, 5, 6, 7, 8 Range: 1, 2, 3, 5	Skills: 1, 2, 3, 4, 6, 7, 8 Range: 1, 2, 3, 4, 5
Bang the Gong			
PNS Literacy Framework (YF)	1.1, 1.2 2.1, 2.2 3.1	(W) 5.1, 5.2, 5.5, 5.6, 5.8, 5.10 (C) 7.1, 8.1	9.1
National Curriculum	working towards level 1		
Scotland (CfE) (P1)	Early level: LIT 0-01A/M/ LIT 0-02A/L/LIT 0-03A/V/LIT 0-04B/C/LIT 0-05D	Early level: LIT 0-01a/LIT 0-11a/LIT 0-20a/ENG 0-12a/ LIT 0-13a/LIT 0-21a/LIT 0-14a/LIT 0-07a/LIT 0-16a/ ENG 0-17a	Early level: LIT 0-01a/LIT 0-11a/LIT 0-20a/ENG 0-12a/LIT 0-13a/LIT 0-21a/LIT 0-21b/LIT 0-26a
N. Ireland (P1)	Attention and Listening: 1, 4, 5 Phonological Awareness: 2, 5 Social use of language: 3, 4, 5 Language and thinking: 1, 2, 4, 5, 6, 7, 11 Extended Vocabulary: 2	Reading: 1, 2, 4, 5, 6, 7, 8, 11, 12 Progression: 1, 3, 4, 5	Writing: 1, 3, 4, 6 Progression: 2, 3, 4, 7, 8
Wales (Foundation Stage)	Skills: 1, 2, 3, 5, 6, 10 Range: 3, 4, 5, 6, 7	Skills: 1, 2, 3, 4, 5, 6, 7, 8, 12, 13 Range: 1, 2, 3, 4, 5	Skills: 1, 2, 3, 4, 6, 8 Range: 1, 2, 3, 4, 5

Curriculum coverage chart

	Speaking, Listening, Drama	Reading	Writing
Jack			
PNS Literacy Framework (YF)	1.1 2.1, 2.2 3.1	Ⓦ 5.1, 5.2, 5.4, 5.5, 5,6, 5.10 Ⓒ 6.1, 7.1, 7.3, 8.1	10.1
National Curriculum	working towards level 1		
Scotland (CfE) (P1)	Early level: LIT 0-01A/M/ LIT 0-02A/L/LIT 0-03A/V/LIT 0-04B/C/LIT 0-05D	Early level: LIT 0-01a/LIT 0-11a/LIT 0-20a/ENG 0-12a/ LIT 0-13a/LIT 0-21a/LIT 0-14a/LIT 0-07a/LIT 0-16a/ ENG 0-17a	Early level: LIT 0-01a/ LIT 0-11a/LIT 0-20a/ ENG0-12a/LIT 0-13a/ LIT 0-21a/LIT 0-21b/ LIT 0-26a
N. Ireland (P1)	Attention and Listening: 1, 4, 5 Phonological Awareness: 2, 5 Social use of language: 3, 4, 5 Language and thinking: 1, 2, 4, 5, 6, 7, 11 Extended Vocabulary: 2	Reading: 1, 2, 4, 5, 6, 7, 8, 11, 12 Progression: 1, 3, 4, 5	Writing: 1, 3, 4, 6 Progression: 2, 3, 4, 7
Wales (Foundation Stage)	Skills: 1, 2, 3, 5, 6, 10 Range: 3, 4,5, 6, 7	Skills: 1, 2, 3, 4, 5, 6, 7, 8 Range: 1, 2, 3, 5	Skills: 1, 2, 3, 4, 6, 8, 9 Range: 1, 2, 3, 4, 5
Quiz			
PNS Literacy Framework (YF)	1.1 2.1, 2.2 3.1	Ⓦ 5.1, 5.2, 5.5, 5.6, 5.7, 5.10 Ⓒ 6.1, 7.1, 8.1	11.1
National Curriculum	working towards level 1		
Scotland (CfE) (P1)	Early level: LIT 0-01A/M/ LIT 0-02A/L/LIT 0-03A/V/LIT 0-04B/C/LIT 0-05D	Early level: LIT 0-01a/LIT 0-11a/LIT 0-20a/ENG 0-12a/ LIT 0-13a/LIT 0-21a/LIT 0-14a/LIT 0-07a/LIT 0-16a/ ENG 0-17a	Early level: LIT 0-01a/ LIT 0-11a/LIT 0-20a/ ENG 0-12a/LIT 0-13a/ LIT 0-21a/ LIT 0-21b/LIT 0-26a
N. Ireland (P1)	Attention and Listening: 1, 4, 5 Phonological Awareness: 2, 5 Social use of language: 3, 4, 5 Language and thinking: 1, 2, 4, 5, 6, 7, 11 Extended Vocabulary:2, 3	Reading: 1, 2, 4, 5, 6, 7, 8, 11, 12 Progression: 1, 3, 4, 5	Writing: 1, 2, 3, 4, 6 Progression:
Wales (Foundation Stage)	Skills: 1, 2, 3, 5, 6, 9 Range: 3, 4,5, 6, 7	Skills: 1, 2, 3, 4, 5, 6, 7, 8 Range: 1, 2, 3, 5	Skills: 1, 2, 3, 4, 6, 8, 11, 12 Range: 1, 2, 3, 4, 5

Curriculum coverage chart

	Speaking, Listening, Drama	Reading	Writing
A Robin's Eggs			
PNS Literacy Framework (YF)	1.1 2.1, 2.2 3.1, 4.1	(W) 5.1, 5.2, 5.5, 5.6, 5.7 (C) 7.1, 8.1, 8.3	10.1
National Curriculum	working towards level 1		
Scotland (CfE) (P1)	Early level: LIT 0-01A/M/LIT 0-02A/L/LIT 0-03A/V/LIT 0-04B/C/LIT 0-05D	Early level: LIT 0-01a/LIT 0-11a/LIT 0-20a/ENG 0-12a/LIT 0-13a/LIT 0-21a/LIT 0-14a/LIT 0-07a/LIT 0-16a/ENG 0-17a	Early level: LIT 0-01a/LIT 0-11a/LIT 0-20a/ENG 0-12a/LIT 0-13a/LIT 0-21a/LIT 0-21b/LIT 0-26a
N. Ireland (P1)	Attention and Listening: 1, 4, 5 Phonological Awareness: 2, 5 Social use of language: 3, 4, 5 Language and thinking: 1, 2, 4, 5, 6, 7, 11 Extended Vocabulary: 2, 3	Reading: 1, 2, 4, 5, 6, 7, 8, 11, 12 Progression: 1, 3, 4, 5	Writing: 1, 3, 4, 6 Progression: 2, 3, 4, 7, 8
Wales (Foundation Stage)	Skills: 1, 2, 3, 5, 6, 12 Range: 3, 4, 5, 6, 7	Skills: 1, 2, 3, 4, 5, 6, 7, 8 Range: 1, 2, 3, 5	Skills: 1, 2, 3, 4, 6, 8, 12 Range: 1, 2, 3, 4, 5

The Zip

C = Language comprehension   **AF** = QCA Assessment focus
W = Word recognition

Phonic Focus:

Phonemes introduced in this book: j, w, y, z, zz

Guided or group reading

Introducing the book

W Encourage children to sound out the title: The Z-i-p . The high frequency words should be read and recognized, not sounded out.

C *(Predicting)* Encourage children to use prediction: *Who is in the picture? What do you think this story is going to be about? What is Dad holding up?*

- Look through the book, talking about what happens on each page. Use some of the high frequency words as you discuss the story (see chart on page 5).

Strategy check

Remind the children to sound out words carefully. If they can't sound out the word, do they already know it from memory?

Independent reading

- Ask children to read the story aloud. Praise and encourage them while they read, and prompt as necessary.

C *(Clarifying)* Ask children why Dad was so keen to jump into the water at the end. Check that children know what a wetsuit is for and how it keeps you warm.

Assessment Check that the children:

- *(AF 1)* use phonic knowledge to sound out and blend the phonemes in words (see chart on page 3)

- *(AF 2)* use comprehension skills to work out what is happening.
- *(AF 1)* Make a note of any difficulties in decoding that the children encounter and of strategies they use to solve problems.

Returning to the text

 (Clarifying) Ask children *Why was Dad getting so hot?*

Assessment *(AF 1)* Discuss any words the children found tricky and talk about strategies used.

Group and independent reading activities

Objective Hear and say sounds in words in the order in which they occur (5.4).

- Ask children to open their books at pages 2–3.
- Tell them that you are going to say all of the sounds in a word. Their job is to say the word and point to it on the page.
- Sound out *f-i-t*. Can the children say and point to the word? How many sounds are there in the word? How many letters?
- Say *w-i-ll*. Can the children say and point to the word? How many sounds are there in the word? How many letters? Remind children that sometimes two letters can show one sound.
- Continue with other words in the book

Assessment *(AF 1)* Can the children say, point to and tell you the number of sounds in a word?

Objective Read some high frequency words (5.9).

- Look at the title page again. Can the children find a word that they *cannot* sound out? (*the*)
- Ask them to count the sounds in the word (2, 3).
- Make a box phoneme frame and find the letters that represent each of the phonemes. Help children to remember the tricky part of the word.

The Zip

Assessment *(AF 1)* Can the children 'quickwrite' the word *the*?

Objective To use phonic knowledge to write regular words (5.8).

- **Ⓦ You will need:** 3 counters for each child, a phoneme frame and a whiteboard to write on.
- Say the word 'job'. Ask the children to push a counter into the phoneme frame for each sound in the word. The children should then say the sounds and the word: *j-o-b job.*
- Ask the children to write the word. Remind them that they will need to make sure that they have represented all of the sounds in the word.
- Ask children to turn to pages 12–13. Can they find the word *job* on those pages? Ask them to check that their spelling is the same as in the book.
- Repeat for other words in the book e.g.: *zip, will, puff, yes, buzz*

Assessment *(AF 1)* Can the children spell all of the words?

Objective Show an understanding of the elements of stories such as characters (8.2).

- **Ⓒ** *(Questioning)* Reread the book, thinking of questions to ask Mum.
- Questions could be about: *did she think it was funny? Where did she get the scissors from? Was she worried about cutting Dad? Why was she happy when Dad jumped into the water?*

Assessment *(AF3)* Check that the children can both ask and answer at least one question.

Speaking, listening and drama activities

Objective Use language to imagine and recreate roles and experiences. (8.3)

- **Ⓒ** *(Imagining)* **You will need:** small world or role play resources for the seaside
- Let children recreate a seaside scene, checking in the book for ideas of what they may need.
- Ask them to create characters out of puppets or dolls. What might they do at the seaside? Again, encourage children to look at the illustrations in the books for ideas.

- If necessary, prompt children with ideas so that they can begin to create a narrative about a day at the seaside.

Assessment Can children create a narrative through role play?

Writing activities

Objective Attempt writing for various purposes (10.1).

- Ask children to write about the story they contributed to at the seaside.

Assessment *(Writing AF1)* Can the children include imaginative details in their writing?

Posh Shops

> **C** = Language comprehension   **AF** = QCA Assessment focus
> **W** = Word recognition

Phonic Focus:

Phonemes introduced in this book: ch, sh, ng, th, x
Context words: Floppy, Kipper, Gran

Guided or group reading

Introducing the book

W Can children read the title? Remind them how to read *sh*.

W Page 1: Can the children find a word with *sh*?

C *(Predicting)* Encourage children to use prediction: *Why do you think the children are shopping?*

- Look through the book, talking about what happens on each page. Use some of the high frequency words as you discuss the story (see chart on page 5).

Strategy check

Remind the children to sound out words carefully. If they can't sound out a word, do they already know it from memory?

Independent reading

- Ask children to read the story aloud. Praise and encourage them while they read, and prompt as necessary.

C *(Summarizing)* Ask children to explain what the book is about in one sentence.

Assessment Check that the children:

- (AF 1) use phonic knowledge to sound out and blend the phonemes in words (see chart on page 3)
- (AF 2) use comprehension skills to work out what is happening

- *(AF 1)* make a note of any difficulties in decoding that the children encounter and of strategies they use to solve problems.

Returning to the text

How many words can the children find with two letters making one sound at the end of the word?

Assessment *(AF 1)* Discuss any words the children found tricky and talk about strategies used.

Group and independent reading activities

Objective Hear and say sounds in words in the order in which they occur (5.4).

You will need: whiteboards

- Ask one of the children to find the word *sang* on pages 14–15.
- Ask children to write the word and draw sound buttons showing the letter-sound correspondence.
- Can they find another word ending in *ng* on pages 14–15? *(hung)*. Children should write it and draw sound buttons again.
- Can they do the same for a word on pages 8–9? *(along)*

Assessment *(AF 1)* Can the children read and spell the word *song*?

Objective Read simple words by sounding out and blending phonemes (5.5).

- Ask children to read pages 4–5. Talk about *sh.* Explicitly teach the strategy of looking whenever there is an *s* in the word to check that it isn't followed by an *h.*
- Write the words *sip* and *ship.* Ask children to read them. What's different? What's the same? Repeat for *sell* and *shell.*
- How many words on these pages have *sh*?
- Ask children to write the words: *sip, ship, shop, miss, wish.* Talk about strategies for spelling the words.

Assessment *(AF 1)* Can the children read and represent all of the sounds in these words?

Posh Shops

Objective To explore and experiment with sounds, words and texts (5.1).

- Read pages 10–13 aloud to the children.
- How many /k/ sounds can they hear? Ask them to put up their hands whenever they hear one.
- Write the words with the /k/ sounds: *Kipper, pick, mix, box, chocs, cash.*
- Ask children to draw sound buttons under the words. How many different ways can they find of representing /k/? (k, ck, x, c). Talk about where in a word each of the ways is most likely to be found (ck and x are most often at the end of a word).

Assessment *(AF 1)* Can the children hear /k/ sounds, even if they can't see a *k*?

Objective To listen to stories and respond with relevant comments, questions or actions (8.1).

C *(clarifying)*

- Ask children simple questions to check on their understanding of the events in the text.

Assessment *(AF 2 and 3)* Can the children respond to your questions using direct evidence and inference?

Speaking, listening and drama activities

Objective Use language to imagine and recreate roles and experiences (4.1)

C *(oral language development)*

- Ask children to make (or to draw) their own shops. All the things sold in each shop must have the same sound in them, so the children will need to look carefully to choose things for their shops. The sound can occur anywhere in the word (e.g. *ship, dish*. The sound does not have to be represented by the same letter pattern in all of the words!)
- Go and visit the children's shops. Ask them to tell you what is in their shop.

- Encourage the children to extend their play as both shoppers and shop-keepers.

Assessment *(AF 2)* Can the children use sentences to explain what kind of shop they have chosen?

Writing activities

Objective Attempts writing for various purposes (9.1).

- Ask children to make a catalogue for the things in their shop. Show them catalogues from shops like Argos, Tesco, Littlewoods etc. to give them a model for their writing.
- Encourage them to use a variety of strategies for spelling the words including using simple dictionaries and classroom displays as well as sounding out the words.

Assessment *(Writing AF2)* Can children produce an appropriate text to match the task?

Bang the Gong

C = Language comprehension **AF** = QCA Assessment focus
W = Word recognition

Phonic Focus:
Phonemes revisited include: ng, sh, ch, j, w, y

Context words: Kipper

Guided or group reading

Introducing the book

W Can children read the title? Remind them that the two letters *ng* join together to make the sound /ng/. Read the title together *B-a-ng the G-o-ng.*

C *(Predicting)* Encourage children to use prediction: *Why is Kipper banging a gong? What kind of sound will it make?*

- Look through the book, talking about what happens on each page. Use some of the high frequency words as you discuss the story (see chart on page 5).

Strategy check

Remind the children to sound out words, remembering *ng* as well as *sh* and *ch*. If they can't sound out a word, do they already know it from memory?

Independent reading

- Ask children to read the story aloud. Praise and encourage them while they read, and prompt as necessary.

C *(Clarifying)* Ask children to explain why Mum wants Kipper to bang the gong.

Assessment Check that the children:

- *(AF 1)* use phonic knowledge to sound out and blend the phonemes in words (see chart on page 3)

- (AF 2) use comprehension skills to work out what is happening
- (AF 1) make a note of any decoding difficulties the children encounter and of strategies they use to solve problems.

Returning to the text

 How many words with *ng* can children find on pages 2–3?

Assessment (AF 1) Discuss any words that the children found tricky and talk about strategies used.

Group and independent reading activities

Objective Recognize common digraphs (5.6).

- Write the words *bang, gong, ping pong, long* on a whiteboard.
- Ask a child to select and read one of the words.
- Let the children draw sound buttons to show how each of the sounds in each word is represented by one or two letters.

Assessment (AF 1) Can the children read and spell the word *song* and *sing*?

Objective Explore and experiment with sounds (5.1).

- Ask children to find the word *fish and chips* on page 6. Can they sound out and blend the phonemes?
- Ask children to read and say the sounds /sh/ and /ch/. Check that the sounds are pronounced differently.
- Write the words *ship* and *chip*. Say 'chip'. Can children point to the correct word?
- Repeat for *shop* and *chop; much, mush*.
- Show the graphemes sh and ch. Say other words aloud (e.g. *wash, watch; sheep, cheap; share, chair*). Can children point to the sound in the word?

Bang the Gong

Assessment *(AF 1)* Can children hear and say the phonemes in words?

Objective To use phonic knowledge to write simple regular words (5.8).

- Ask children to write the word *shop*. Support them, if necessary.
- Ask them to write the words *shed, ship* and *wish*.
- Now ask them to write *chip*, *rich* and *long*. Do they remember which graphemes are needed in each of the words?

Assessment *(AF 1)* Can the children spell the words?

Objective To show an understanding of the elements of stories such as main character.

C *(Questioning)*

- Talk about the characters in the book. Who is the main character? How do children know? Is it Mum or Kipper?
- Encourage children to ask questions about the story to explore whether Mum or Kipper is more important.

Assessment *(AF 2 and 3)* Can the children identify the main character in a story?

Speaking, listening and drama activities

Objective Use talk to organize, sequence and clarify thinking (1.2)

C *(Clarifying; imagining)*

- Page 1: *Look at the picture. What is Mum cooking?* Discuss which meal she is making. Look at clues in the pictures- the food on the table, the clothes she is wearing and the clock.
- Look at the next meal on page 6. Ask the children the same questions: which meal is Mum making now? What is the evidence?
- When is the next meal? Can children identify it on page 12-13. Which meal is Mum making now?
- Discuss how Mum feels when everyone is late to her meals. What idea does she come up with?

Assessment *(AF 2)* Can the children use clues in the text and pictures to infer which meal Mum is serving through the course of the day?

(AF3) Can they use clues in the text and pictures to infer how Mum is feeling?

Writing activities

Objective Begin to form simple sentence sometimes using punctuation (9.1).

- Ask the children to look at page 10 and talk about what Mum is thinking about.
- Give them speech bubbles. Ask them to write a sentence to say what Mum is thinking.

Assessment *(AF1)* Can children begin to form a simple sentence and write recognizable words using phonic knowledge?

Jack

> **C** = Language comprehension **AF** = QCA Assessment focus
> **W** = Word recognition

Phonic Focus:

Phonemes introduced in this book: qu
Phonemes revisited include: ch, sh, j, x
Context words: Kipper, Floppy, cock-a-doodle-do

Guided or group reading

Introducing the book

(W) Can children read the title? J-a-ck.

(W) Introduce the word *quick* on page 1. Talk about the sound represented by *qu*. Sound out the word: *qu-i-ck*.

(C) *(Predicting)* Encourage children to use prediction: *Where are the family? What are they doing here?*

- Look through the book, talking about what happens on each page. Use some of the high frequency words as you discuss the story (see chart on page 5).

Strategy check

Remind the children to sound out words carefully, remembering *ch, sh* and *qu*. If they can't sound out a word, do they already know it from memory?

Independent reading

- Ask children to read the story aloud. Praise and encourage them while they read, and prompt as necessary.

(C) *(Clarifying)* Ask children to explain why everyone is saying shhh! at the end.

Assessment Check that the children:

- *(AF 1)* use phonic knowledge to sound out and blend the phonemes in words (see chart on page 3)

- *(AF 2)* use comprehension skills to work out what is happening
- *(AF 1)* make a note of any decoding difficulties the children encounter and of strategies they use to solve problems.

Returning to the text

Ⓦ Can children read the word that the cockerel is crowing at the end of the book?

Assessment *(AF 1)* Discuss any words the children found tricky and talk about strategies used.

Group and independent reading activities

Objective recognize common digraphs (5.6).

Ⓦ **You will need:** plastic or wooden letters c, s, k, q, u, h and whiteboards with pens.

- Place *qu* on the table and ask children if they remember the consonant phoneme. Say it together.
- Can children make the word *quick,* using the qu and writing the rest of the word? Say the word together and count the phonemes (3). Check that children recognize which phonemes are represented by which letters.
- Repeat for *quiz, quack, quit,*

Assessment *(AF 1)* Can children read and spell the word *quill*?

Objective Hear and say sounds in words in the order in which they occur (5.4).

- Write the words *chick* and *chicken.*
- Ask children to read the words. Discuss what is the same and what is different. Can children clap the words?
- Look at *chicken* again. Demonstrate how to split the word into two syllables *chick-en.* Show children how to sound out and blend the word syllable by syllable and then combine the complete syllables, rather than trying to blend the whole word. Offer this as a strategy for reading longer words.

Assessment *(AF 1)* Can children read the words *rock* and *rocket* using this strategy?

Objective To use phonic knowledge to write simple regular words (6.1).

- **You will need:** a whiteboard with a three phoneme phoneme-frame drawn on it.
- Can the children write 'Jack'?
- Ask them first to sound-talk the word J-a-ck, then to write the word, one sound at a time into the phoneme frame. They should then say and blend the sounds to check for their own accuracy.
- Repeat for *dish, six, pick, Chip*
- When you have talked about the words 'quickwrite' them.

Assessment *(AF 1)* Can the children spell the words?

Objective To show an understanding of the elements of stories such as main character (7.3).

(Questioning)

- Ask different children who they think the characters are in the story.
- Make labels for each of the characters- including Jack.
- Rank the name labels in order of importance in the story.
- Encourage children to ask questions, based on the text, to challenge other children's suggestions. If necessary, model some questions.

Assessment *(AF 3)* Can the children ask and answer questions to justify their ranking of the characters?

Speaking, listening and drama activities

Objective Show an understanding of the elements of stories, such as main character, sequence and openings (7. 3).

C *(Summarizing)*

- Look at the picture on page 1. Discuss what happened *before* the story started. Ask one child to state what you have decided. Give that child a card saying *First*.
- Look at segments of the book. After each segment, discuss a one sentence summary and give children cards saying *Then, After that, Next, Finally*.
- Put the children in order and ask each one to state their summary of the events in the story.

Assessment *(AF 2)* Can the children use language effectively to explain their part of the story?

Writing activities

Objective Attempts writing for various purposes (10.1).

C *(Summarizing)*

- Ask children to make a sentence which tells you the most exciting part of the story.
- Help them to write their sentence and illustrate it. Encourage them to spell as many words as possible correctly using their phonic knowledge. Let them make plausible attempts at harder words.

Assessment *(AF1)* Can children use their phonic knowledge to make plausible attempts at more complex words?

Quiz

C = Language comprehension   **AF** = QCA Assessment focus
W = Word recognition

Phonic Focus:
Phonemes introduced in this book: th
Phonemes revisited include: qu, ng, x, w, sh, ch, j
Context words: Kipper

Guided or group reading

Introducing the book

W Can children read the title? Read the title together *Qu-i-z*

W Turn to pages 2–3. Point out the words *with, thin, thick*. Show children the *th* and demonstrate the two sounds it represents. Ask children to copy. Sound-talk the three words: *w-i-th, th-i-n, th-i-ck*.

C *(Predicting)* Encourage children to use prediction: *What kind of game are they playing? What might happen at the end?*

- Look through the book, talking about what happens on each page. Use some of the high frequency words as you discuss the story (see chart on page 5).

Strategy check
Remind the children to sound out words carefully, remembering that sometimes two letters can represent one sound. If children can't sound out a word, do they already know it from memory?

Independent reading

- Ask children to read the story aloud. Praise and encourage them while they read, and prompt as necessary.

C *(Clarifying)* Ask children to explain what happened at the end of the book.

Assessment Check that the children:
- *(AF 1)* use phonic knowledge to sound out and blend the phonemes in words (see chart on page 3)
- *(AF 2)* use comprehension skills to work out what is happening
- *(AF 1)* make a note of any decoding difficulties the children encounter and of strategies they use to solve problems.

Returning to the text

Ⓦ Look carefully at the words *thin* and *this*. Can children draw sound buttons for the words? What is the same and what is different for these words?

Assessment *(AF 1)* Discuss any words the children found tricky and talk about strategies used.

Group and independent reading activities

Objective Recognize common digraphs (5.6).

Ⓦ **You will need:** flashcards of words containing *th*. e.g. *with, the, this, that, then, them, they; thin, thick, thing, thud, moth* (also *bath* and *path* if children pronounce them with a short 'a')

- Place *this* and *thin* on the table. Challenge the children to sort the words so that they make sets showing the two different pronunciations of *th*.
- Ask children to sound talk and then read the words before they make their choice. Support the children in trying out two different pronunciations of *th*.

Assessment *(AF 1)* Can children read and sort all of the words?

Objective To read some high frequency words (5.7).

- Show the children the words *them* and *this*. Read the words.
- Ask children to use sound buttons to show the (3) phonemes in *each* of the words and to identify which letters represent each one.
- Repeat for *they*. Can the children identify the tricky letters in *they*?

Quiz

- When you have talked about the words 'quickwrite' them.

Assessment *(AF 1)* Can the children spell the words?

Objective Use phonic knowledge to write regular simple words (6.1).

- **You will need:** list of 10 words containing /k/. e.g a selection of: quick, quiz, quack, quill; cat, can, canal, cup; kid, kit, king, kiss; back, tick, luck, deck.
- Ask each child to make four sets: a set of words with *qu,* a set with *c,* a set with *k* and a set with *ck.*
- Read the words aloud. Ask children to sound-talk them, then decide which set to write each word in.

Assessment *(AF 1)* Can children sound-talk the words, make good choice about representing /k/ and spell the words accurately?

Objective Ask questions about*, who, how* and *what* (7.3).

C *(Questioning)*

- Model asking a question: *Who was the giraffe*? Or *How did Biff make the giraffe*? Or *What was Biff?*
- Ask children to frame their own questions about the text.
- Let them talk to a response partner so that each can both ask and answer questions.

Assessment *(AF 2)* Can the children ask and answer good questions about events in the text?

Speaking, listening and drama activities

Objective Interact with others, negotiating plans and activities (3.1).

C *(Imagining)*

- Look again at the quiz in the book. Tell the children that you're going to play a game like this one.
- In secret, give each child a picture or model of an animal.

- Ask the child to think about words and actions they will need to show the animal. Remind them that the speaker can't say the animal's name in your version of the game, allow people who are guessing to say the name.
- Once the children have played the game using the animals you gave them, invite them to think of their own animals then describe and move like the animal.

Assessment Can the children use ideas from the text to talk about and show their own animals?

Writing activities

Objective Begin to form simple sentence sometimes using punctuation (11.1).

- Help children to make a booklet by folding a piece of paper in half.
- On the front of the booklet, they should write one or two simple sentences describing an animal.
- Inside the booklet they should draw a picture of their animal.

Assessment *(AF1)* Can children begin to form a simple sentence and write recognizable words using phonic knowledge?

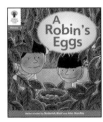

A Robin's Eggs

> **C** = Language comprehension   **AF** = QCA Assessment focus
> **W** = Word recognition

Phonic Focus:
Phonemes introduced in this book: v
Phonemes revisited include: w, sh, ng, th, qu
Context words: Mrs May

Guided or group reading

Introducing the book

W Can children read the title? Talk about the apostrophe. Explain what it means. Sound out the title of the book together: *R-o-b-i-n-s E-gg-s*.

C *(Predicting)* Encourage children to use prediction: *What are the children doing? Why do Biff and Chip have to get bats? What might they find?*

- Look through the book, talking about what happens on each page. Use some of the high frequency words as you discuss the story (see chart on page 5).

Strategy check

Remind the children to sound out words carefully, remembering that sometimes two letters can represent one sound.

Independent reading

- Ask children to read the story aloud. Praise and encourage them while they read, and prompt as necessary.

C *(Clarifying)* Talk about what is happening on pages 14–15.

Assessment Check that children:

- *(AF 1)* use phonic knowledge to sound out and blend the phonemes in words (see chart on page 3)
- *(AF 2)* use comprehension skills to work out what is happening

- *(AF 1)* make a note of any decoding difficulties the children encounter and of strategies they use to solve problems.

Returning to the text

- **(W)** Can children find words with double letters in them? (e.g. *egg, tell, Biff*.) Talk about the fact the *ck* is used instead of *kk*. Can children add any words to their list? (*chicks, quick, unlock*)

Assessment *(AF 1)* Discuss words the children found tricky and talk about strategies used.

Group and independent reading activities

Objective Recognize common digraphs (5.6).

- **(W) You will need:** flashcards with the sounds: *zz, gg, ss, ll, ck, ff, ch, sh, th, ng, qu*.
- Place all of the flashcards on the table. Remind the children that all of these have two letters but only make one sound. Ask children to say the sounds.
- Talk about where in a word the pairs of letters come in a word. Clarify that double letters (including ck) never occur at the beginning of a word.
- Ask children to write words containing each of the letter patterns. Explore where in the word children choose to write the letters.

Assessment *(AF 1)* Can children read and spell the words?

Objective Read simple words by sounding out and blending the phonemes (5.5).

- **(W) You will need:** plastic or wooden letters: c, h, s, t, n, g, k, i, a, p
- Make the word *chin*. Read it together, checking which phonemes are represented by which letters.
- Ask children which sound they could change to make a different word (e.g. *thin, shin, chip*). Can the children read the new word?
- Can they change one sound in the new word to make another word?
- Continue to explore ways of changing just one sound to make a new word.

Assessment *(AF 1)* Can children suggest new words and read the words they make?

Objective To read some high frequency words (5.7).

(W) Show the children the words *we* and *she.* Read the words.
- Which is the tricky letter each time? Compare the words with *the.* What is the same and what is different?
- Knowing these two words, challenge children to spell: *me, be, he.*
- When you have talked about the words 'quickwrite' them.

Assessment *(AF 1)* Can the children spell the words?

Objective To show an understanding of the elements of stories such as sequence ((8.3).

(C) *(Summarising)* Make name labels for each of the characters in the book.
- Ask the children to re-read the book and to list the names in the order in which they appear (make *class* a word to represent the rest of the class).
- Can the children tell you what the role of each person was as they appeared in the story? *Who saw the nest? Who helped? How? What did they do or see?*

Assessment *(AF 2 and 3)* Can the children sequence the events in the story and explain who did what to move the events on?

Speaking, listening and drama activities

Objective Use language to imagine and recreate roles and experiences (4.1).

(C) *(Imagining)* Give each of the children a character label (including *class* and a silent part *robin*). Ask them to reread the book so that they know what their character's role is.
- Let the children act out the story, speaking the words from the book.
- Recreate the webcam of the nest, using toys in the classroom.

Assessment *(AF 2)* Can the children use sentences appropriately for their part in the play?

Writing activities

Objective Attempt writing for different purposes using features of different forms (10.1).

(W) Ask children to draw the sequence of webcam pictures from memory.
- Then ask them to write a sentence beside each picture.

Assessment *(Writing AF1)* Can children write their sentences fluently, using full stops?